CONTENTS

ONE OF THOSE WHO SAID

YES

MARIAROSA GUERRINI O.S.A.

ONE OF THOSE
WHO SAID

YES

the story of a call

St Paul Publications

Original title: UNO DI QUELLI CHE HA
DETTO SI. Produced by the Federation of
Augustinian Nuns, Italy. First published
in 1982 by Editrice Rogate, Roma. Seventh
reprint 1985. All rights reserved.

Translated by Vincent Siletti SSP
English text lettering: Mary Lou Winters DSP

St Paul Publications
Middlegreen, Slough SL3 6BT, England

English language edition copyright
© 1986 St Paul Publications, Slough
ISBN 085439 257 2

Printed by Dotesios Printers Ltd, Trowbridge, Wiltshire

PRE...... DESTINATION

'Before I formed you in the womb
   I knew you;
   and before you were born
   I consecrated you...'.

Jer 1, 5

WHEN I WAS A BABY

As soon as I was born
I desired that pure,
spiritual milk that makes one grow.

cf 1 Pt 2,2

AND I GREW UP.....

... and became
strong in spirit.

cf Lk 1, 80

DREAMS AND.......IDEALS

I kept thinking:

When I am a grown-up....
I will save the world!

THE CALL

One day........

Your radiance shone upon me...
and put my blindness to flight.
...You touched me, and I became
inflamed with desire of your love.

St Augustine

RESISTANCE.....

I tried to say 'no', but
I was seized by Christ....

FRIGHT........ AND FEAR

THE VOICE OF THE LORD:

Do not be afraid:
I HAVE CHOSEN...

'...what is foolish in the world
to shame
the wise,

_____

...what is weak
in the world
to shame the strong,

_____

...what is low and
despised in the world,
even the things that
are not,
to bring to nothing
the things that are...'

1 Cor 1, 27

_____

IT TAKES DARING!........

.....the unconscious daring
of young children.

AND SO IT HAPPENED
THAT I SAID:

.... AND LET GO OF MYSELF

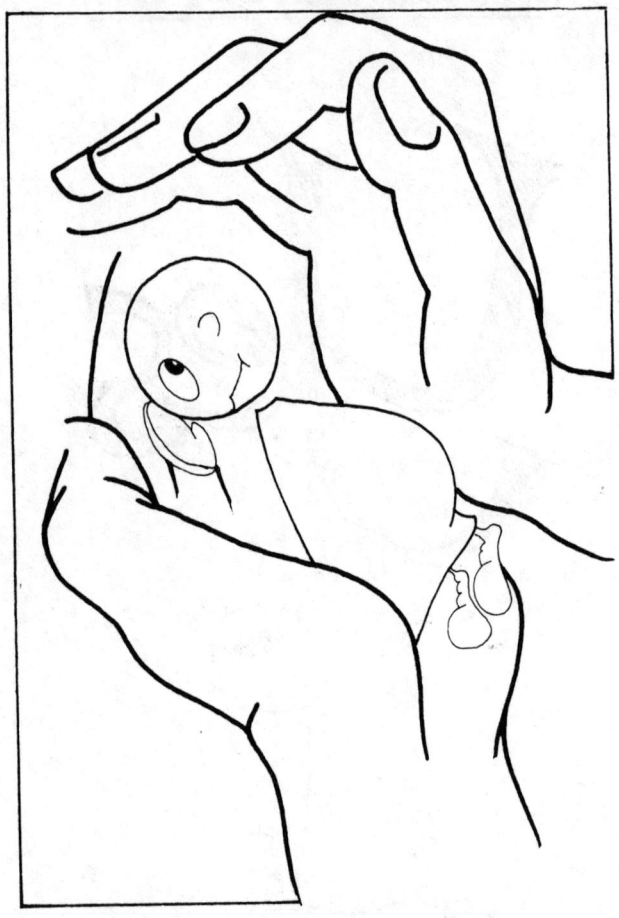

'I know in whom I put my trust...'

cf 2 Tim 1, 12

'My refuge and my fortress,
my God, in whom I trust'.

Ps 91, 2

AT THE BEGINNING I WAS SO HAPPY

I am not afraid of anything:

'The Lord made my feet
like hinds' feet
and set me secure
on the heights.'

2 Sam 22,34

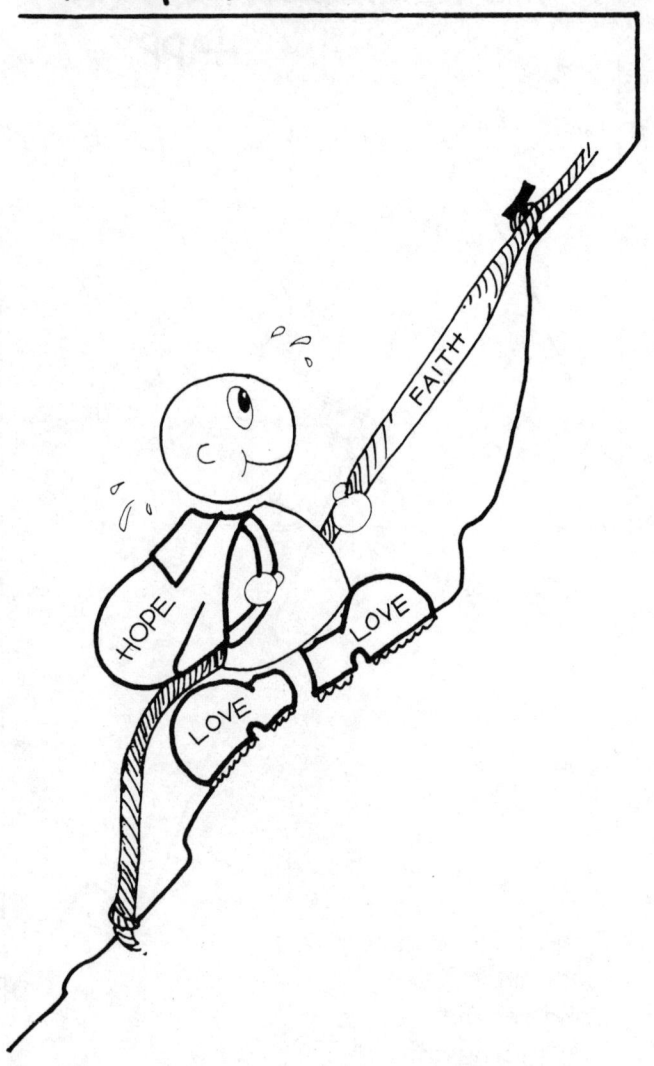

ON THE WAY..... WITH GOD

'He will bear me
as a man bears his son,
in all the way that
you have to go'.   cf Deut 1, 31

'I will walk
in the light
of His Word'.

cf Ps 86, 11

TRAINING PERIOD

There are two ways of dealing with

TEMPTATIONS:

1 Either... GO OFF LIKE A SHOT

2 Or... FACE THE ENEMY

'Even though an army
encamp against me ...'.

'My heart
would not
fear'.
Ps 27, 3

' When I am weak...

... then I am strong!'
2 Cor 12,10

AND SO...
TO ENCOURAGE ME
THEY BEGAN
TO GIVE ME
ADVICE

ADVICE
IN ORDER TO GET THERE*!?!*

AT THE SCHOOL
OF THE SPIRIT

STRIP YOURSELF
OF EVERYTHING......

"YES EVERYTHING!"

DO NOT FORGET:

TO REACH
   GOD'S HEIGHTS....

Do you want to build a tower?
Think first of the foundations:
   HUMILITY...

St Augustine

...and if that 'ME' becomes
an encroachment...
Give it a kick, and...
LIVE IN HEAVEN.

St Augustine

41

METHODS AND TECHNIQUES

for Meditation
Self-denial
Etc.

WILL THESE BE
OF ANY USE?

...the one, essential thing is to let
'the only Light' shine upon you, and wait...

REMAIN...........IN HIS PRESENCE

to learn
that the Christian life
is a life in two...
'Me and Him'

43

KEEP IN BALANCE

When thoughts weigh you down and anguish overwhelms you...

MORALS

S.O.S.

HELP

...it is a sign of balance and maturity to do something about it...

THE TEACHING OF JESUS

'Take up your cross
and follow me...'

cf Lk 9, 23

...if you cannot carry it,
it will carry you...

... and if the 'load' becomes too heavy,
there is always a 'Father'
to give you rest.

cf Mt 11, 28

HOWEVER, IT IS NOT ENOUGH TO KNOW THE RULES OF GOD'S GAME TO AVOID HARD WORK AND TO REMOVE OBSTACLES....
IT HAPPENS TO ALL OF US DOESN'T IT?!?...

STATES OF MIND:

When fatigue of mind or body
'shatters' your day.....

.....the slightest thing
will knock you down.....

.....BEING CRUSHED

'You beset me...
and lay your hand upon me...'

Ps 139,5

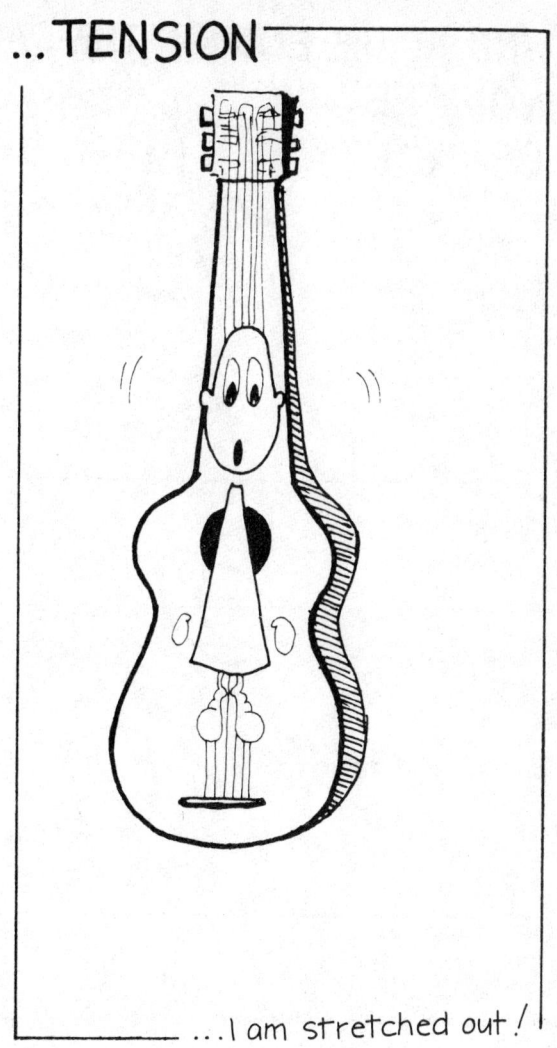

...I am stretched out!

AND AT THE END OF THE DAY
YOU FEEL
BEATEN

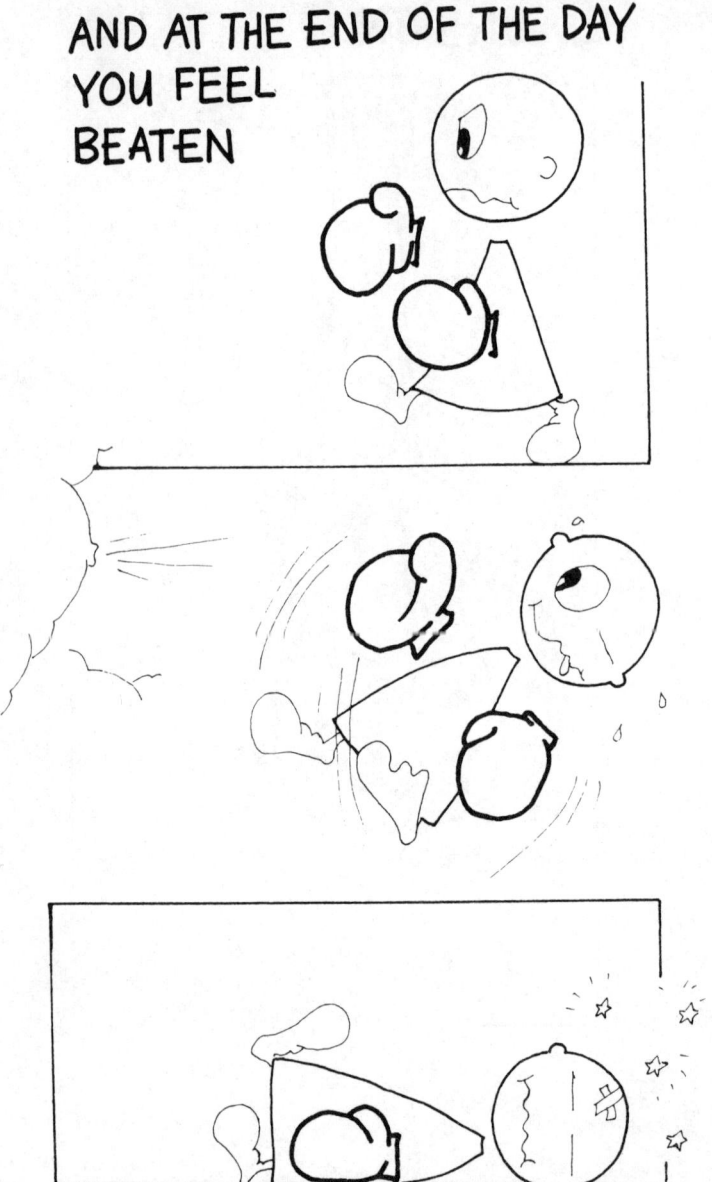

POINTS OF VIEW

I am running straight.....

.....it's the world that.....
goes round !

61

In solitude and void
the spirit grows in strength.

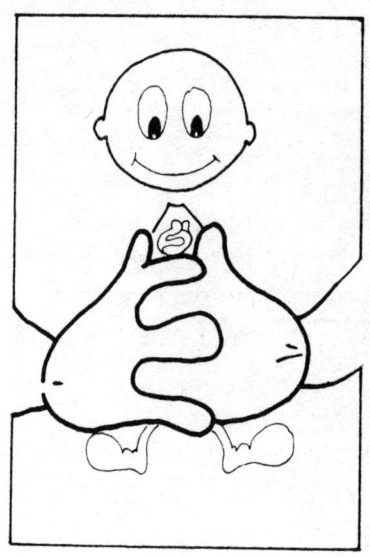

Even if the world
collapses.....
keep calm,
relax.....
'like a baby
in its mother's arms'.

Ps 130,2

Lord,
the water
is reaching
my knees...

Lord,
the water
is up to
my neck...

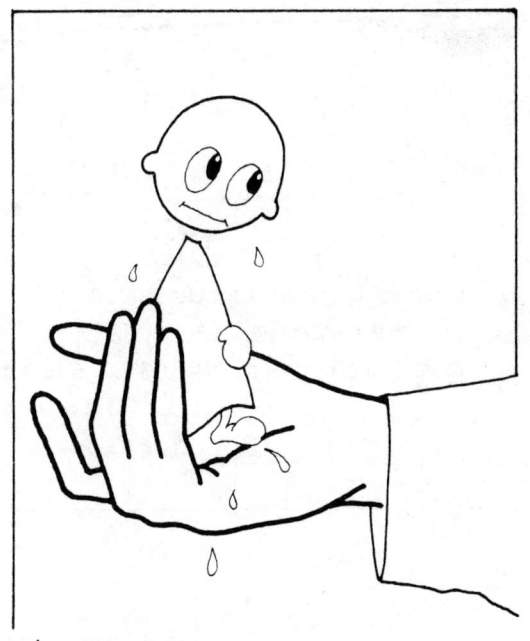

Jesus took him
by the hand and said:

'MAN OF LITTLE FAITH,
WHY
DID YOU DOUBT?'

Mt 14. 29f

'They will bear you up
   on their hands, lest you
   dash your foot against a stone'.

Ps 91, 12

'...They are all around me ...
lifting me up!'

cf Lk 19, 43

INTERCESSION
OF THE SAINTS

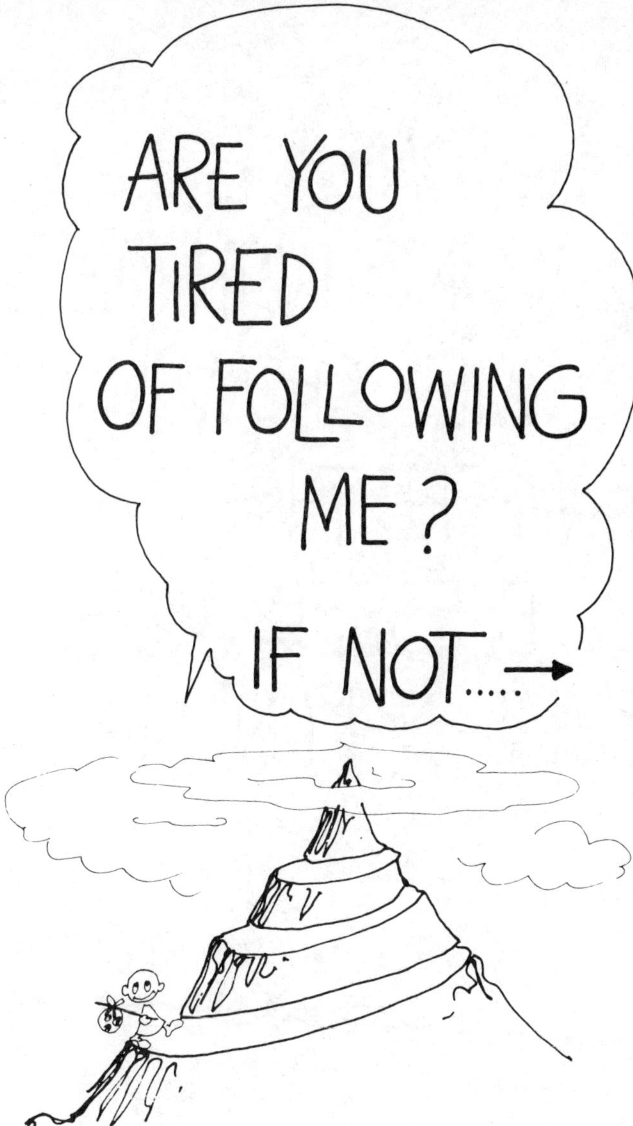
ARE YOU
TIRED
OF FOLLOWING
ME?
IF NOT.....

SINCE THE FIRST
ANNOUNCEMENT OF
THE GOSPEL
A GREAT NUMBER OF MEN
AND WOMEN
HAVE SAID THEIR **YES**
TO CHRIST
WHO CALLED THEM.
THEY CHOSE THE PRIESTHOOD,
THE RELIGIOUS LIFE,
THE MISSIONARY LIFE,
AS SCOPE AND IDEAL
OF THEIR EXISTENCE.

POPE JOHN PAUL II

NOW.....
IS YOUR HOUR.
ARE YOU
AFRAID ?

POPE JOHN PAUL II

REMEMBER THE WORDS OF JESUS:

'Pray the Lord of the harvest,
to send labourers to his harvest'.

Mt 9, 38

'...to the ends of the earth...'

Acts 1,8

MY NOVICIATE

Knocked out

1... 2...3...4...5...

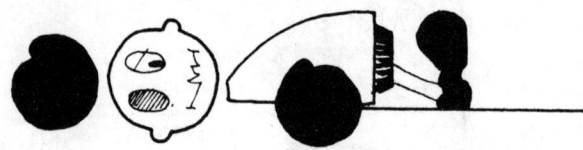

'A time of struggle?...'

AT THE END OF A LONG, UNENDING YEAR,
ONE DAY I SAW THE SUPERIOR
AND THE BROTHERS DISAPPEAR
BEHIND A DOOR.....

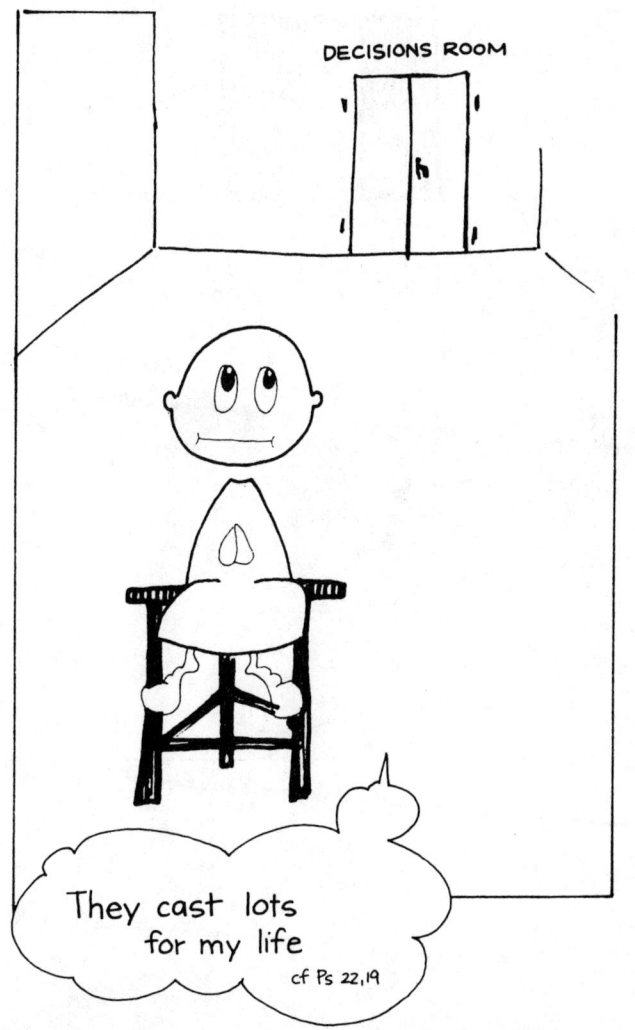

CHASTITY is...

BALANCE
between earth and... heaven.

...and 'seeking none other'
than God.

POVERTY is...

being a gift
for others.

...and 'handing over'
   mind and heart.

OBEDIENCE is...

...letting oneself be led

...it is Faith

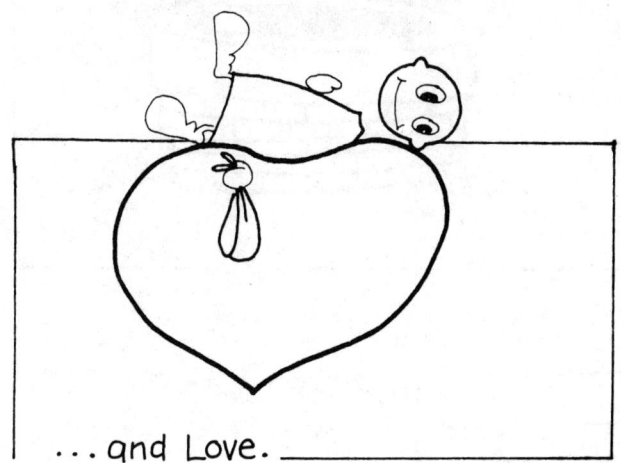

...and Love.

IN A WORD
THE VOWS ARE.....

MADNESS

but... for love!

DAILY MEETING:

Come to see me. I live...
in your heart!

ADORATION

From all directions He draws me
towards the centre.....

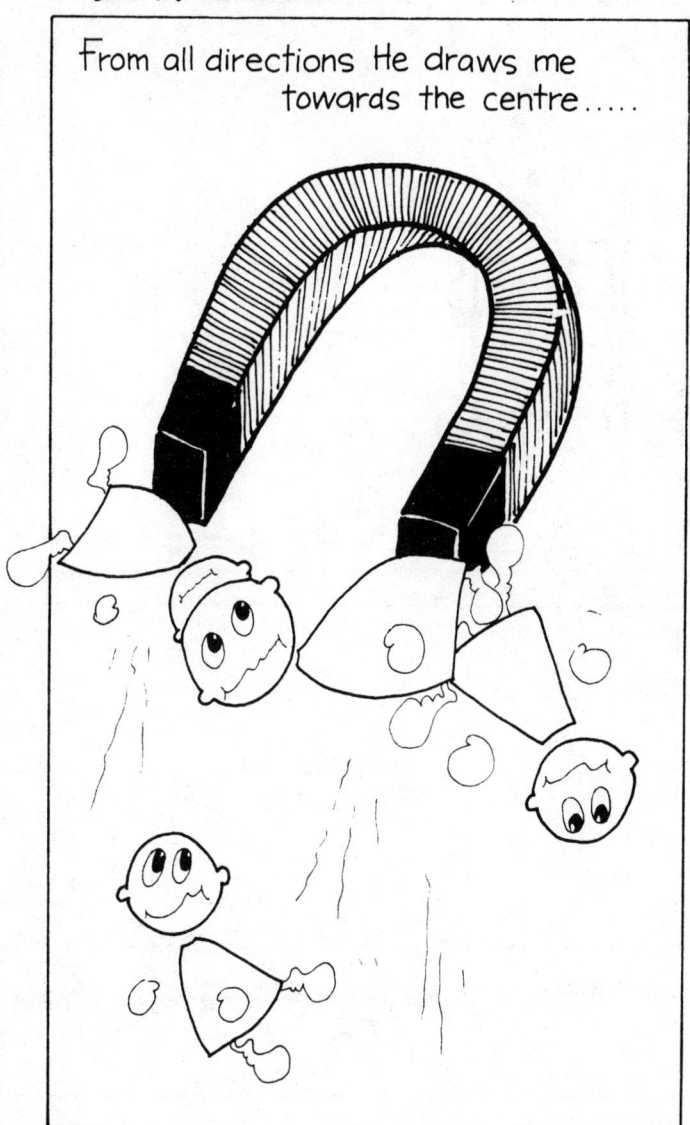

ECSTASY...

and...

reality......

STEPS.....OF LOVE:

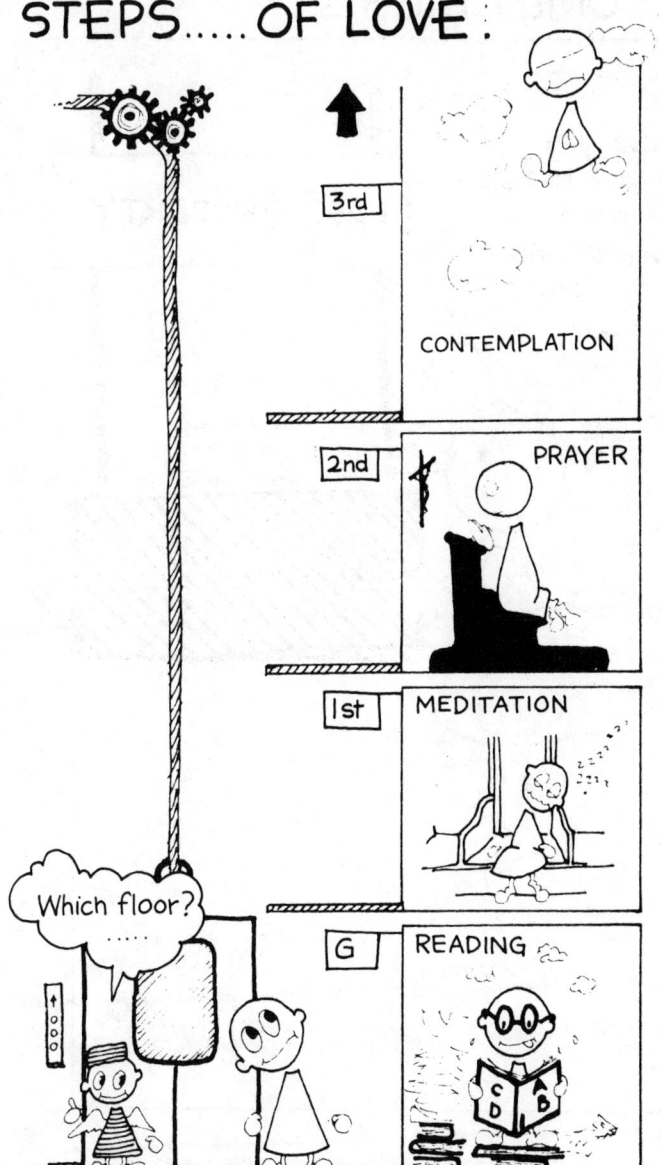

WORK and......

PRAYER

Ding dong

Ding dong

At the sound of the bell the servant of God interrupts whatever he is doing......

DIVINE
OFFICE

FRIENDSHIP and.....

.....they will be 'God's Family'
insofar as they are
united in LOVE...

ST AUGUSTINE

..... SOLIDARITY

'You should support the other
just as the other should support you'....

ST AUGUSTINE

otherwise...
this is what happens!

'Bear one another's burdens.'

Gal 6,2

TOGETHER
WE CAN SUSTAIN
THE WORLD

EVANGELISATION

AND....

HUMAN ADVANCEMENT

..... SEASONING
FOR THE EARTH

'You are the salt of the earth'.

Mt 5.13

..... LIGHT
FOR HUMANKIND

'You are the light
of the world.'

Mt 5,14

EXTENSION
OF JESUS.....

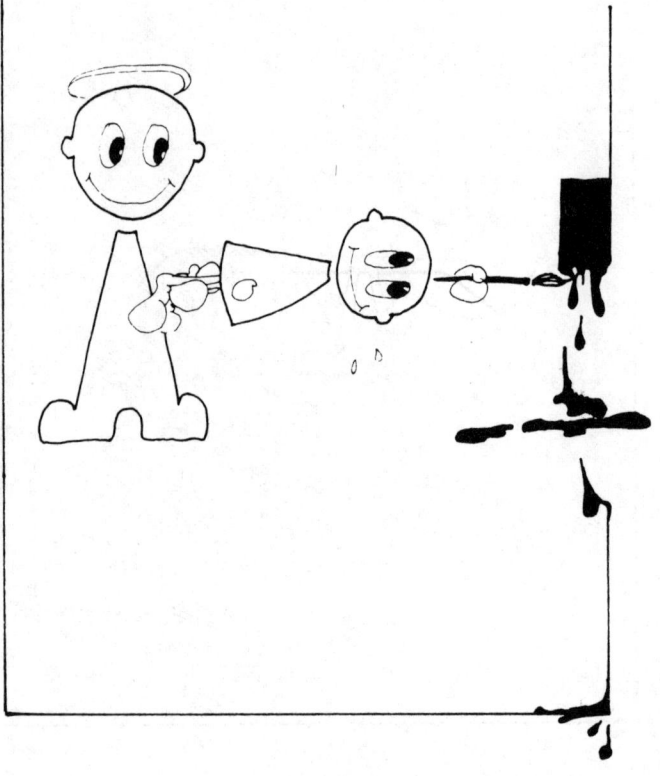

WORLD'S BAKERY

AND

YOU TOO

LORD JESUS,
GIVE THE ABUNDANCE
OF YOUR LIFE
TO ALL THOSE
YOU HAVE CALLED
TO YOUR SERVICE,
ESPECIALLY THE
YOUNG MEN AND WOMEN.
ENLIGHTEN THEM IN THEIR CHOICE,
HELP THEM IN THEIR DIFFICULTIES,
GIVE THEM STRENGTH TO BE FAITHFUL,
MAKE THEM READY AND STRONG
TO OFFER THEIR LIVES
FOLLOWING YOUR EXAMPLE,
SO THAT OTHERS TOO
MAY HAVE LIFE.

POPE JOHN PAUL II

GO, THEN, LIKE FIRES BURNING WITH HOLINESS AND BEAUTY.....

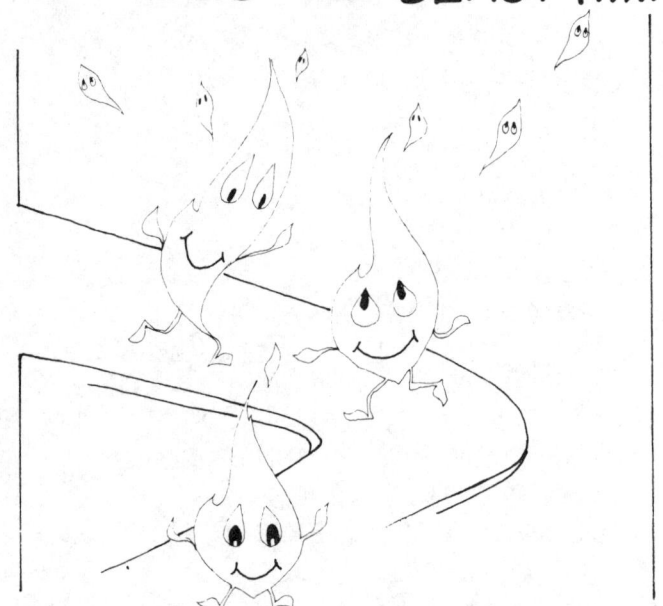

GO ALL OVER THE WORLD AND LEAD ALL PEOPLES TO THE LIGHT.

ST AUGUSTINE

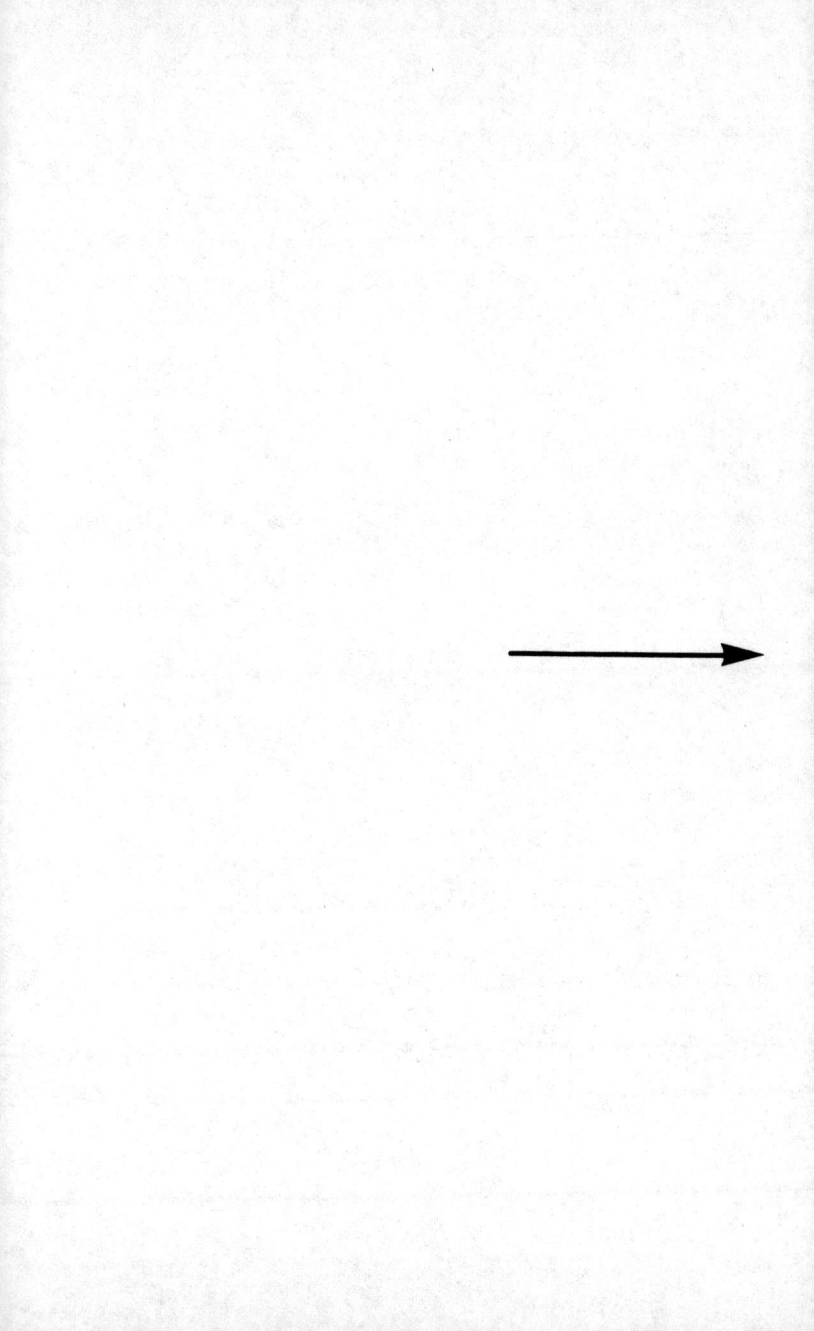

Have you read:

DO YOU LOVE ME?

A GENIAL WAY OF PRESENTING THE GOSPEL....

THE CALL OF THE GOSPEL AND PETER'S RESPONSE OF LOVE ILLUSTRATED WITH AN ADMIRABLE SENSE OF HUMOUR....

The fascinating adventure of following Jesus and the sweeping message of his teaching are, here, narrated by Peter, the apostle who experienced the unutterable joy of the answer to the call of the Lord.

Peter's is the story of impassioned love — unique. Reading its pages, everyone will be able to grasp the criterion and the measure of true and real love.

Have you also read:

LATE HAVE
I LOVED YOU

Publisher's note

This little book
has been produced
and published by
the priests and brothers
of the Society of St Paul
and the Daughters of St Paul,
two of the Congregations of
the Pauline Family whose mission
is to proclaim the Gospel
all over the world
through the media of
social communication.